# GLUCOFIT

## MAKING THE WORLD DIABETIC FREE

MANISHA

# Contents

# Preface

Diabetes mellitus (DM) is one of the most common non-communicable diseases (NCDs) globally. Diabetes mellitus is also known as premaha or madhumeha. It is most commonly found in many economically developing and newly industrialized countries. Diabetes mellitus is a disorder that affects the body's ability to make or use insulin. Insulin is a hormone produced in the pancreas that helps transport glucose (blood sugar) from the bloodstream into the cells so they can break it down and use it for fuel. It has been narrated in Ayurveda that, the long periods of physical inactivity, laziness, sleeping for long hours, excess use of food which is heavy to digest like dairy products, aquatic and marshy animals, sugar/ jaggery preparations, fresh grains etc. and similar foods that increase kapha are generalized causes of prameha \ diabetes mellitus. Diabetes is a metabolic disease that occurs when your blood sugar also known as blood glucose level is too high. The term high blood glucose is also known a HYPERGLYCAEMIA.

According to Ayurveda, a body is in its healthiest state if and when *Vata*, *Pitta* and *Kapha* are in balance. Any imbalance will lead to health ailments. Diabetes is essentially cause by the imbalance of *Pitta* in the body. "*Pitta* promotes fire and when the fire begins to diminish in the body, diabetes begins to take shape. It therefore becomes important to get *Pitta* back in balance by practicing breathing techniques that promote *agni* in the body - like *Agnisar Kriya* and *Suryabhedi Pranayam* - and by including foods that will maintain blood sugar levels and balance *Pitta* in the body," noted Yogacharya Anoop, Mediyoga.

Ayurveda is an ancient medicine practice that is emerging in the United States as a complementary and alternative treatment for chronic illness. Type 2 diabetes is a chronic illness that has major long-term implications for individuals suffering from the disease as well as the health-care system as a whole. Modifications in diet, exercise, and lifestyle are all important factors in successful treatment of type 2 diabetes and are incorporated into the ancient Indian medicinal practice of Ayurveda.

Ayurveda connects physical (prakriti), spiritual (purusha), and physiologic processes to promote a healthy relationship between the mind, body, and soul. The primary goal of Ayurveda is to maintain equilibrium between the 5 basic elements (Panchamahabhutas) of earth, water, fire, air, and ether or vacuum within oneself through the theory of the 3 life forces or doshas. The doshas consist of vata, which correlates to ether and air, pitta, which represents fire, and kapha, which equates to the elements of earth and water. Vata, pitta, and kapha are the doshas of the body, while rajas, tamas, and satva are the doshas of the mind.

# CHAPTER ONE

# DIABETES MELLITUS The Comprehensive and Oldest Disorder

## BACKROUND

Diabetes is a greek word which means go through and mellitus means sweet. It is a shortened version of the full name diabetes mellitus. Joseph von mering and oskar minkowski in 1899 are discovered that the removal of the pancreas from a dog allowed it to develop diabetes.

Diabetes mellitus (DM) is probably one of the oldest diseases known to man. It was first reported in Egyptian manuscript about 3000 years ago. In 1936, the distinction between type 1 and type 2 DM was clearly made. Type 2 DM was first described as a component of metabolic syndrome in 1988. Type 2 DM (formerly known as non-insulin dependent DM) is the most common form of DM characterized by hyperglycemia, insulin resistance, and relative insulin deficiency. Type-2 DM results from interaction between genetic, environmental and behavioral risk factors. A 2017 report Trusted Source from the Centers for Disease Control and Prevention (CDC) found that 30.3 million adults in the United States have diabetes. The report also estimated that another 84.1 million U.S. adults have pre-diabetes.

## WHAT IS BLOOD GLUCOSE?

Blood glucose is a simple sugar and it is a component of many carbohydrates. The formula of glucose is $C_6H_{12}O_6$ and it is also known as six carbon sugar. Glucose (sugar) is our body's main source of energy. For example- gasoline is to a car. Glucose come from the food we eat (carbohydrate). One of our body organ ''liver'' is responsible for stores glucose and release it into your blood. SOURCE OF GLUCOSE- Food product like yogurt, milk, potato, fruits, sugar, rice e.t.c.

## What is Diabetes mellitus?

Diabetes mellitus (DM) is one of the most common non-communicable diseases (NCDs) globally. Diabetes mellitus is also known as premaha or madhumeha. It is most commonly found in many economically developing and newly industrialized countries. Diabetes mellitus is a disorder that affects the body's ability to make or use insulin. Insulin is a hormone produced in the pancreas that helps transport glucose (blood sugar) from the bloodstream into the cells so they can break it down and use it for fuel. It has been narrated in Ayurveda that, the long periods of physical inactivity, laziness, sleeping for long hours, excess use of food which is heavy to digest like dairy products, aquatic and marshy animals, sugar/ jaggery preparations, fresh grains etc. and similar foods that increase kapha are generalized causes of prameha \ diabetes mellitus. Diabetes is a metabolic disease that occurs when your blood sugar also known as blood glucose level is too high. The term high blood glucose is also known a HYPERGLYCAEMIA.

**In Ayuveda "Madhumeha"** is used as a term for Diabetes. One of the other most common reason causing diabetes is changed and this modern lifestyle.

Genetic inherited of diabetes lead down to a type of Diabetes mellitus which is inheritically taken from parents and older families already suffering from Diabetes mellitus genetically. Diabetes is a serious chronic condition in which it causes resulting from a deficiency of the pancreatic hormone INSULIN and an irregularity in the release of glucagon, a polypeptide hormone. Under these conditions, the pancreas is continually stressed to secrete its hormone in order to eliminate the excess glucose from the blood.

**PANCREAS - Natural Factory of Essential Hormones**
**Main Function: Secretion of Essential Hormones**
**Cluster Named: Langer-hans**
**Name of Cells: Alpha-Cells, Beta-Cells & Delta Cells**
**Hormones Produced: Insulin and Glucagon**

**Weight In Adult: 80Grams**

Pancreas is a flattened organ of body and located posterior and slightly inferior to the stomach. The main function of pancreas is to make essential hormones that are needed to breakdown and get energy from the food.

The pancreas has an endocrine function because it release juices directly into the bloodstream, and it has an exocrine function because it release juices into ducts.

## ANATOMIC CONSIDERATIONS

The anatomical relationships between the pancreas and organs surrounding it in the abdomen. The pancreas is a retroperitoneal organ and does not have a capsule. The second and third portions of the duodenum curve around the head of the pancreas. The spleen is adjacent to the pancreatic tail. The regions of the pancreas are the head, body, tail and uncinate process.

The distal end of the common bile duct passes through the head of the pancreas and joins the pancreatic duct entering the duodenum. For this reason, pathologic processes of the pancreas, such as a cancer at the head of the pancreas or swelling and/or scarring of the head of the pancreas due to pancreatitis, can lead to biliary system obstruction and injury. Because of its posterior position, the pancreas is usually protected from trauma. However, it is just anterior to the vertebral column, and severe blunt trauma to the upper abdomen as might occur from a steering wheel in an auto accident can "crush" the pancreas against the vertebral column and cause severe injury.

The arterial blood supply to the pancreas is from two major arteries supplying the abdominal organs, the celiac and superior mesenteric arteries. Because of the dual blood supply, ischemia to the pancreas from vascular obstruction is uncommon. Venous drainage of the pancreas is via the splenic vein and the superior mesenteric vein draining into the portal vein. The splenic vein runs along the body of the pancreas. Diseases, such as pancreatitis and pancreatic cancer, can involve the splenic vein leading to its thrombosis and vascular engorgement of the spleen due to the obstruction of venous blood flow.

The pancreas is innervated by both the parasympathetic and sympathetic nervous systems. The efferent parasympathetic system is contained within the branches of the vagus nerve that originates in the dorsal vagal complex (tenth cranial nerve nucleus) of the brain. The terminal branches of the vagus synapse with intrapancreatic ganglia. The postganglionic fibers innervate both exocrine and endocrine structures that are described in the next section. The sympathetic innervation originates in the lateral grey matter of the thoracic and lumbar spinal cord. The bodies of the postganglionic sympathetic neurons are located in the hepatic and celiac plexuses. The postganglionic fibers innervate blood vessels of the pancreas.

## ISLETS OF LANGER-HANS

The endocrine portion of the pancreas consists clusters of cells called ISLETS OF LANGER-BANS . In Langer-bans three types of cells that is – ALPHA CELLS, BETA CELLS AND DELTA CELLS.

**Alpha-cells** is responsible for secretion of glucagon which acts to raise blood sugar level.

**Beta-cells** is responsible for secrete the hormone insulin which acts to lower the blood sugar level and the third one is delta cells which secrete GHIH ( growth hormone inhibiting hormone ) that is responsible to inhibit the secretion of insulin and glucagon.

## What are Beta-cells?

Beta cells are cells that make insulin, a hormone that controls the level of glucose (a type of sugar) in the blood. Beta cells are found in the pancreas within clusters of cells known as islets. In type 1 diabetes, the body's immune system mistakenly destroys the beta cells. When the beta cells die, the body no longer can produce enough insulin to regulate blood-glucose levels, and this can lead to serious health complications, even death, without treatment. It is generally understood that inflammation plays a vital role in beta-cell destruction.

## Functions of Beta-Cells

The main function of a beta cell is to produce and secrete insulin - the hormone responsible for regulating levels of glucose in the blood.

**1.9 INSULIN – The Natural Doctor Hormone Controlling Diabetes**
**Main Function: Control Higher Blood Suger Level**
**Cluster Named: Langer-bans**

**Name of Cells: Beta-Cells**
**Hormones Type: Silent Poison Produced By Body**
Insulin is the "key" that allows glucose to enter the cells. Without this key, glucose stays in the bloodstream and the cells can't use it for energy. Instead, the glucose builds up in the blood and spills over into the urine.

Insulin is a hormone made by one of the body's organs called the pancreas. Insulin helps your body turn blood sugar (glucose) into energy. It also helps your body store it in your muscles, fat cells, and liver to use later, when your body needs it.

Insulin helps keeps your blood sugar level from getting too high (hyperglycemia) or too low (hypoglycemia).

It starts working after several hours after injection and works for approximately 24 hours. If necessary, it is often used in combination with rapid- or short-acting insulin.

### Types of insulin

There are many type of insulin.

**Rapid-acting insulin:** These take between 5 and 15 minutes to have an effect. However, the size of the dose impacts the duration of the effect. Assuming that rapid-acting insulin analogs last for 4 hours is a safe general rule.

**Short-acting insulin:** The onset of regular human insulin is between 30 minutes and an hour, and its effects on blood sugar last around 8 hours. A larger dose speeds up the onset but also delay the peak effect of regular human insulin.

**Intermediate-acting insulin:** This takes between 1 and 2 hours to onset, and reaches its peak within 4 to 6 hours. It can last over 12 hours in some cases. A very small dose will bring forward the peak effect, and a high dose will increase the time NPH takes to reach its peak and the overall duration of its effect.

**Long-acting insulin:** While long-acting insulin is slow to reach the bloodstream and has a relatively low peak, it has a stabilizing "plateau" effect on blood sugar that can last for most of the day. It is useful overnight, between meals, and during fasts.

### How insulin work?

After you eat, your blood sugar (glucose) rises. This rise in glucose triggers your pancreas to release insulin into the bloodstream. Insulin travels through the blood to your body's cells. It tells the cells to open up and let the glucose in. Once inside, the cells convert glucose into energy or store it to use later. Without insulin, your body can't use or store glucose for energy. Instead, the glucose stays in your blood.

## Functions of insulin

**Insulin** is an important part of metabolism and necessary for turning glucose into energy and distributing it to cells all throughout your body. **Insulin** helps the liver, muscle, and fat cells to store the glucose you don't need right away, so it can be used for energy later.

Insulin is a hormone which plays a number of roles in the body's metabolism.

Insulin regulates how the body uses and stores glucose and fat. Many of the body's cells rely on insulin to take glucose from the blood for energy.

## Clinical Features of Diabetes Mellitus

Common symptoms of diabetes include:

- Polyuria - increased urination
- Polyphagia - excessive appetite
- Polydyspia - excessive thirst
- Unusual weight loss or weight gain
- Fatigue
- Nausea, perhaps vomiting
- Blurred vision
- In women, frequent vaginal infections
- In men and women, yeast infections
- Dry mouth
- Slow-healing of sores or cuts in the skin / mucosa
- Itching of the skin, especially in the region of groin or genitals

## Premonitory signs and symptoms

- Sweet taste in the mouth
- whitish urine with sweetish odor
- Attraction of insects and ants to the urine / person
- Dryness in mouth, palate and throat
- Thirst/drowsiness
- Excessive sweating and foul smelling of the body
- Lethargy

- Unhygienic body
- Excessive deposition of waste products in palate, tongue and teeth etc.
- Matting of the hair
- Abnormal appearance of the urine
- Numbness and burning sensation in hands and feet etc

## Complications of diabetes -

Complications due to diabetes are a major cause of disability, reduced quality of life, and death. Diabetes is a systemic disease that affects most of the body organs especially heart, blood vessels, kidneys, eyes and nerves.

Diabetes increases patients' risk for many serious health problems. In men, it is responsible for erectile dysfunction, low testosterone levels and emotional factors such as depression, anxiety or stress–that can interfere with sexual feelings. In women, heart disease is the leading cause of death in women with diabetes numerous complications may arise as a result of diabetes, which include the following:

- Cardiovascular diseases:
- Diabetic nephropathy:
- Diabetic eye disease:
- Diabetic neuropathy:

**Types of diabetes –**
There are mainly 3 types of diabetes.

- Type 1
- Type 2
- Gestational diabetes

## TYPE 1 DIABETES

In type 1 diabetes, the pancreas stops making insulin. To help the body's cells use the glucose, a child with type 1 diabetes mellitus (DM) must receive insulin by injection (shot).

**What Happens in Type 1 Diabetes**

The cause of diabetes is not known. Some experts believe diabetes is inherited (runs in families), but the genetics are not clearly understood. Diabetes does not always run in families. The body mistakes the cells that produce insulin for foreign cells. The body then destroys these cells. This is called an auto-immune process. Although something in the environment may trigger the disease, there are no known ways to prevent type 1 diabetes in children.

**Early Signs of Type 1 DM are**

- Weight loss or poor weight gain, even if eating large amounts of food
- More thirst than usual
- Enuresis (bed wetting)
- Frequent urination
- More urine than usual
- Feeling tired all the time

## Type 2 DIABETES

Another type of diabetes is type 2, non-insulin dependent diabetes mellitus (NIDDM). Type 2 diabetes is more common than type 1. About 9 out of 10 people with diabetes have type 2. Type 2 DM used to occur mostly in adults, but is becoming increasingly more common in children. It is associated with obesity. NIDDM usually starts after 40 years of age. People with type 2 diabetes usually produce enough of their own insulin, but their bodies don't use it right. Type 2 may be controlled by weight loss or with insulin and/or oral medicine.

**Early Signs of Type 2 DM Are -**

**Frequent urination -**

When blood sugar levels are high, the kidneys try to remove the excess sugar (glucose) by filtering it out of the blood. This can lead to a person needing to urinate more frequently, particularly at night.

**Increased thirst -**

The frequent urination that is necessary to remove excess sugar( glucose) from the blood can result in the body losing additional water. Over time, this can cause dehydration and lead to a person feeling more thirsty than usual.

**Always feeling hungry –**

The digestive system breaks food down into a simple sugar called glucose, which the body uses as fuel. In people with diabetes, not enough of this glucose moves from the bloodstream into the body's cells. As a result, people with type 2 diabetes often feel constantly hungry, regardless of how recently they have eaten.

**Slow healing of cuts and wounds -**

High levels of sugar in the blood can damage the body's nerves and blood vessels, which can impair blood circulation. As a result, even small cuts and wounds may take weeks or months to heal. Slow wound healing also increases the risk of infection.

**Tingling, numbness, or pain in the hands or feet –**

In people with type 2 diabetes, this can lead to pain or a sensation of tingling or numbness in the hands and feet. This condition is known as neuropathy, and it can worsen over time and lead to more serious complications if a person does not get treatment for their diabetes.

## GESTATIONAL DIABETES

Gestational diabetes is high blood sugar (glucose) that develops during pregnancy and usually disappears after giving birth. It can happen at any stage of pregnancy, but is more common in the second or third trimester.

**Early sign of gestational diabetes -**

- Obesity
- A history of gestational diabetes in a previous pregnancy
- A family history of type 2 diabetes and having pre-diabetes.

# CHAPTER TWO

# PRAMEHA ROGHA In accordance To Ayurveda

### <u>Background</u>

According to Ayurveda, a body is in its healthiest state if and when *Vata*, *Pitta* and *Kapha* are in balance. Any imbalance will lead to health ailments. Diabetes is essentially cause by the imbalance of *Pitta* in the body. "*Pitta* promotes fire and when the fire begins to diminish in the body, diabetes begins to take shape. It therefore becomes important to get *Pitta* back in balance by practicing breathing techniques that promote *agni* in the body - like *Agnisar Kriya* and *Suryabhedi Pranayam* - and by including foods that will maintain blood sugar levels and balance *Pitta* in the body," noted Yogacharya Anoop, Mediyoga.

Ayurveda connects physical (prakriti), spiritual (purusha), and physiologic processes to promote a healthy relationship between the mind, body, and soul. The primary goal of Ayurveda is to maintain equilibrium between the 5 basic elements (Panchamahabhutas) of earth, water, fire, air, and ether or vacuum within oneself through the theory of the 3 life forces or doshas. The doshas consist of vata, which correlates to ether and air, pitta, which represents fire, and kapha, which equates to the elements of earth and water. Vata, pitta, and kapha are the doshas of the body, while rajas, tamas, and satva are the doshas of the mind.

### Background of "Prameha Rogha" In Ayurveda

Originating in ancient India, Ayurveda is a traditional medicinal practice with roots tracing back to 1000 BC. It was first categorized as a religious or spiritual medicine, but during the 6th- to 4th-century BC, the religious healing approach lost popularity, and it began to become systematically organized. Translated from Sanskrit to mean "science of life,"

According to Ayurveda, a body is in its healthiest state if and when *Vata*, *Pitta* and *Kapha* are in balance. Any imbalance will lead to health ailments. Diabetes is essentially cause by the imbalance of *Pitta* in the body. "*Pitta* promotes fire and when the fire begins to diminish in the body, diabetes begins to take shape. It therefore becomes important to get *Pitta* back in balance by practicing breathing techniques that promote *agni* in the body - like *Agnisar Kriya* and *Suryabhedi Pranayam* - and by including foods that will maintain blood sugar levels and balance *Pitta* in the body," noted Yogacharya Anoop, Mediyoga.

Ayurveda connects physical (prakriti), spiritual (purusha), and physiologic processes to promote a healthy relationship between the mind, body, and soul. The primary goal of Ayurveda is to maintain equilibrium between the 5 basic elements (Panchamahabhutas) of earth, water, fire, air, and ether or vacuum within oneself through the theory of the 3 life forces or doshas. The doshas consist of vata, which correlates to ether and air, pitta, which represents fire, and kapha, which equates to the elements of earth and water. Vata, pitta, and kapha are the doshas of the body, while rajas, tamas, and satva are the doshas of the mind.

According to Ayurveda, striking equilibrium between the doshas corresponds to good health. Each living being has a tendency toward certain doshas structurally and physiologically, and such imbalances may lead to disease. Ayurvedic practitioners make use of individualized diet, exercise, and lifestyle as well as procedural, medicinal, and herbal prescriptions in order to bring their patient's doshas into optimal balance. The primary medicines used in Ayurveda are derived from plants; however, metal, mineral, as well as marine- and animal-derived materials are also used. Currently, the Indian government controls all policy development, growth, and implementation of Ayurveda programs. The World Health Organization began understanding the benefits of traditional medicines in the late 1970s, helping to improve the global acceptance of Ayurveda.

Ironically, popularity of Ayurveda in the United States grew after Westerners became increasingly aware of the inability to cure certain chronic illnesses while recognizing the side effects of Western medications. Integrative medicine, which combines Eastern and Western practices, is on the rise with the hope of rebalancing health and wellness in Western population. Many case reports have shown the use of traditional medicine such as Ayurveda as being beneficial and even curative to a number of chronic illnesses including but not limited to arthritis, low back pain, hypertension, sciatica, migraine, neuropathy, parkinsonism, thyroid imbalances, liver disease, dysmenorrheal, polycystic ovarian syndrome, irritable bowel syndrome, asthma, allergies, eczema, depression, anxiety, and many others. The use of Ayurveda in type-2 diabetes, a chronic, yet treatable disease, has shown marked improvement on patient outcomes in numerous case reports. Type-2 diabetes involves a lack of sensitivity to insulin and the subsequent inability of the body to regulate blood glucose levels. Type-2 diabetes is the most common form of diabetes in the United States and primarily results from unhealthy lifestyle choices. According to the American Diabetes Association, when possible, type-2 diabetes should be treated with exercise, diet, and lifestyle modifications.

However, progression to oral hypoglycemic agents and insulin will likely be necessary at some point during the course of a patient's disease process as their pancreas is unable to keep up with amount of insulin necessary to compensate for the body's resistance to insulin. Risk factors for type 2 diabetes are widely known and include being overweight or obese (body mass index [BMI] of 25 or higher), family history of diabetes, lack of physical activity, poor diet, including excessive calorie consumption, low fiber intake, high consumption of saturated and trans fats, high glycemic load, high glycemic index, cigarette smoking, and alcohol consumption. Measuring the individual dietary and lifestyle factors as indicators for type 2 diabetes, they found individuals with a low risk of the disease were under the BMI classification of overweight (<25.0), engaged in vigorous or moderate exercise for 30 minutes each day, were nonsmokers, consumed 5 g or more of alcohol per day with no defined upper limit of alcohol consumption because study subjects did not consume more than 45 g of alcohol per day, and ate a diet high in cereal fiber and low in trans-fat. They collected responses to questionnaires for nearly 85 000 female nurses and did follow-up for 16 years. Their research suggests that the majority of cases of type-2 diabetes could be prevented by weight loss, regular exercise, modification of diet, abstinence from smoking, and the consumption of limited amounts of alcohol with weight control appearing to offer the greatest benefit.

Overtime, high blood glucose has major complications, including damage to the heart, blood vessels, kidneys, eyes, peripheral nerves, digestive system, wound healing ability, and sexual response and leads to complications during pregnancy. A small reduction in hemoglobin A1c

(HbA1c) of less than 1% has been shown to have a clear association with improved patient outcomes regardless of treatment with Western pharmaceuticals or alternative and complementary medicine. Because both the cause and treatment of type-2 diabetes are related to diet and lifestyle, the ancient medicinal practice of Ayurveda, which is rooted in diet and lifestyle, is a promising traditional approach to the treatment of type-2 diabetes. Due to the large portion of the United States population suffering from type-2 diabetes and the serious complications that result from the disease, health-care costs resulting from this illness are astronomical. Thus, the use of Ayurveda in treating type-2 diabetes should benefit more than just those who are suffering from diabetes.

## Factors Causing Premaha

आस्यासुख स्वप्नसुखंदधीनि ग्राम्यौदकानूपरसाः पयांसि।
नवान्नपान्न गुडवैकृतं च प्रमेहहेतुः कफकृच्च सर्वम्॥१॥

Indulgence in sitting on soft cushions for long periods ( thus avoiding physical activity) , sleeping for long hours, use of curds , flesh of animals of domestic , aquatic or of marshy places , milk ( and its preparations ) , fresh grains , fresh water , puddings made of jaggery / sugar ( and its other products ) and all other similar factors which bring about increas of kapha in the body are the causes for prameha ( polyurea/ diabetes)

## Varieties of Prameha

मेदश्च मांसं च शरीरजं च क्लेदं कफो बस्तगितः प्रदूष्य ।
करोति मेहान् समुद्रीर्णमरुणसितानेव पित्तं परदिष्य चापि॥२॥
क्षीणेषु दोषेष्ववकृष्य धातून् सदूष्य मेहान् करुतेनलिश्च ।
साध्याः कफोत्था दश, पित्तजाः षड् याप्या, न साध्यः पवनाच्चतुष्कः ॥
समकुरयित्वाद्वषिमकुरयित्वान्महात्ययत्वाच्च यथाक्रमं ते ॥

Kapha undergoing increase , vitiates the medas ( fat) , mamsa ( muscle) and kleda ( body fluids) , draws them to the urinary bladder and produces prameha: similarly the pitta affects them , vata also brings about vitiation in them and produce prameha. The ten kinds produced by kapha are easily curable, six kinds by pitta are controllable and four kinds by vata are incurable respectively; because of similarity (in respect of the causative dosas and the vitiated dhatus having identical properties); dissimilarity (

in respect of causative dosa and vitiated dhatus having different properties ) and grave consequences (vataja types giving rise to severe complications quickly).

कफः सपत्तितः पवनश्च दोषा, मेदोऽस्रशक्रराम्बुवसालसीकाः ।
मज्जा रसौजः पशितिं च दूष्याः, प्रमेहणि वशितरिव मेहाः ॥४॥

In all the twenty varieties of prameha , vata , pitta and kapha together form the causitive dosas ; medas ( fat) , asrk ( blood) , sukra ( semen) , ambu ( body fluids ) , vasa ( muscle fat ) , lasiki ( tissue fluid ) , majja ( marrow ) , rasa ( lymph ) , ojas ( essence of all the dhatus ) and pisita ( muscle tissue ) are the dusya , ( affected tissues).

## Symptomes of Prameha

दन्तादीना मलाढ्यत्वं प्रागरूपं पाणिपादयोः ।
दाहश्चक्किणता देहे तट्टू स्वाद्वास्यं च जायते ॥५॥

Premonitory symptoms are accumulation of dirt on the teeth ( mouth , eyes , nose , ears ) , feeling of burning sensation in the plams and soles , stickiness of the skin all over the body , thrist and a sweet taste in the mouth.

## Characteristic Features of Prameha

सामान्य लक्षणं तेषां प्रभूतावलिमूत्रता । दोषदूष्यावशिषेऽपि तत्संयोगवशिषतः ॥६॥
मूत्रवर्णादभिदेन भेदो मेहेषु कल्य्यते । (वा.नि.अ. १०)

Increased quantity and turbidity of urine are the characteristic features. Due to the combination of dosas and dusyas ; different colour are seen in the urine and pramehas ( diabetes ) are classified depending upon the colour of the urine , etc .

## Diagnosis of Urine for Prameha

अच्छं बहुसति शीतं नर्गिगन्धमदुकोपमम् ॥७॥
महत्यडुकमेहेन कर्चिदिावलिपच्चिछिलिम् । इक्षो रसमविात्यर्थं मधुरं चेक्षुमेहतः ॥८॥
सान्द्रीभवेत् पर्यृषति सान्द्रमेहेन मेहति । सुरामेही सुरातुल्यमपर्यच्छमधो घनम्
॥९॥

संहृष्टरोमा पष्टिने पष्टिवद्बहुलं सतिम् । शुक्राभं शुक्रमशिरं वा शुक्रमेही पुरमेहति ॥१०॥

मूत्राण्नू सकितामेही सकितारूपणिो मलान् । शीतमेही सुब्रहुशो मधुरं भृशशीतलम् ॥११॥

शनैः शनैः शनैर्मेही मन्दं मन्दं पुरमेहति । लालातन्तुयुतं मूत्रं लालामेहेन पच्छिलिम् ॥१२॥

Clear , copious , white , cold , odourless , with little turbidity and gressiness , almost resembling water are the features of urine in Udakameha.

Urine , very sweet like the juice of sugarcane is found in Iksumeha.

Urine kept undisturbed for sometime in a pot assuming thickness is seen in sandrameha.

In Surameha the urine resembles sura ( alcoholic beverage prepared with flour ) with clear fluid on top and sediments at the bottom.

In Pistameha ,the urine appears thick as though mixed with flour and is white in colour , the patient experiences horripulations often.

In Sukrameha , the urine resemble semen or even be mixed with it .

In Sikatameha , the urine contains small particles resembling sand .

In Sitameha , the urine is copious , sweet in taste and vry cold in touch.

In Sanairmeha , the elimination of urine is very frequent and very slow.

In Lalameha , the urine resembles saliva with appearance of threads and is sticky.

( these ten varities are predominantly kaphaja.

गन्धवर्णरसस्पर्शः क्षारेण क्षारतीयवत् । नीलमेहेन नीलाभं कालमेही मसीनभिम् ॥१३॥

हारद्रिमेही कटुकं हरद्रिासनंभिं दहत् । वस्त्रि माञ जष्ठिमेहेन मछष्ठिासललिोपमम् ॥१४॥

वनिमुणां सलवणं रक्ताभं रक्तमेहतः । (था.नि.अ.१०}]

In Ksarameha , the urine resembles solution of alkali in smell , colour , taste and touch.

In Nilameha it is blue , in kalameha it is like charcoal.

In Haridrameha , the urine is pungent and deep yellow and the patient experiences burning sensation during urination.

In Manjisthameha , the urine is foul smelling and resembles decoction of manjistha ( Rubia cardifolia).

In Raktameha the urine is having foul smell , hot , salty taste and red in colour like that of blood.

( the above six varities are predominantly pittaja.)

वसामेही वसामशिरं वसाभं मूत्रयेन्मुहुः ॥१५॥

मज्जाभं मज्जमशिनं वा मज्जमेही मुहुर्मुहुः । कषायं मधुरं रूक्षं क्षौद्रमेहं वदेद्बुः ॥१६॥

हस्ती मत्त इवाजस्रं मूत्रं वेगवविर्जतिम् ।

सलसीकं वविद्धं च हस्तिमेही प्रमेहता ॥१७॥ (वा.न.अ. १०)

In Vasameha , the urine is mixed with muscle fat or appears like that and is voided frequently.

In Majjameha , the urine is mixed with marrow or appears like that and is voided frequently.

In Ksaudrameha , the urine looks like a decoction , is sweet , and non – sticky.

In Hastimeha , the person passes urine continuously like an elephant in heat , slowly ( without pressure )and it is mixed with lasika ( tissue fluid).

( The above four varities are predominantly vataja).

## Complications of Prameha

बस्तिमेहनयोस्तोदो मुष्कावदरणं ज्वरः ।

दाहस्तृष्णाऽम्लिका मूच्छा वड्भिेदः पत्तिजन्मनाम् ॥१९॥

Pain in the urinary bladder and penis , cracks in the skin of the scrotum , fever , felling of burning sensation , thrist , sour erectations , faintings and diarrhoea are the complications of pittaja pramehas.

## Hereditary Prameha

जातः प्रमेही मधुमेहिनी वा न साध्य उक्तः स हि बीजदोषात् ।

ये चापि केचित्किुलजा वकिारा भवन्ति तांस्तान् प्रवदन्त्यसाध्यान् ॥२२॥

(च.च.अ.६)

A person who is born with prameha (hereditary diabetes ) or a person who is suffering from madhumeha are said to be incurable because of defect in genesis itself before their birth . Likewise, many other hereditary diseases also are said to be incurable.

## Other Edges of Prameha

अन्तोन्नता तु तद्रूपा नमिन्मध्या शरावकिा । गौरसर्षपससंस्थाना तत्प्रमाणा च
सर्षपी 1। २९ ।।

सदाहा कूर्मससंस्थाना ज्ञेया कच्छपकिा बुधैः । जालिनी तीव्रदाहा तु मांसजालसमावृता
।।३०।।

अवगाठरुजाक्लेदा पृष्ठे वाऽप्युदरेऽपि वा । महती पडिका नीला विनता नाम सा स्मृता
।।३१।।

महत्यल्याचचिता ज्ञेया पडिका चापि पुतुरणिी । मसूराकृतिसंस्थाना वज्ज्ञेया तु मसूरिका
।। ३२।।

रक्ता सिता स्फोटचिता दारुणा त्ववलजी भवेत् । विदारीकन्दवद्वृत्ता कठनिा च विदारिका
।।३३।।

विद्रिधरेलक्षणैर्युक्ता ज्ञेया विद्रिधकिा तु सा । ये यन्मयाः स्मृता महास्तेषामेतासत्
तन्मयाः ।। ३४।।

(सु.नि.अ. ६)

Saravika resembles a saucer with elevated edges and depressed centre ;
sarsapika is similar to white mustard seeds in colour and size; kacchapika
resembles a tortoise shell and causes sensation of burning; jalini is shaped
like a seive of muscle fibres and will have severe burning sensation.

Vinata appears on the back or abdomen , with hard , blue , big sized
tubercles associated with pain and exuation.

Putrini is a bigger ulcer with small ulcers spread around.

Masurika is ulcer in the shape and size of masura dala ( pea ) , Alaji is red
or white in colour , bursts out and very dreadful; Vidarika is round and hard
like tuber of vidari.

Vidradhika will be having all the features of an abscess.

शरावकिा कच्छपकिा जालिनी विनिताऽलजी । मसूरिका सर्षपकिा पुतुरणिी सविदारिका
।।२७।।

विद्रिधश्चितेति पडिकाः प्रमेहोपेक्षया दश । सन्धिर्मर्मस्जायन्ते मांसलेषु च धामस्।।
२८।। (वा.नि.अ. १०)

Saravika , kacchapika , jalini , vinata , alaji , masurika , sarspika , putrini
, vidarika and vidradhika are the ten types of tubercles ( corbuncles) in
relation to pramehas . They appear on joints , vital parts and other fleshy
parts of the body.

विना प्रमेहमप्येता जायन्ते दुष्टमेदसः ।

तावच्चैता न लक्ष्यन्ते यावद्वास्तुप्ररगिरहः ।।३५।। (च.सू.अ. १७)

These ulcers might occur , even without prameha ( diabetes) in persons
in whom the medas ( fat / adipose tissue ) has undergone abnormal change

; but it cannot be recognised till it gets localised in specified parts.

गुदे हृद्वि शिरस्यंसे पृष्ठे मर्मस्चोत्थतिाः ।
सोपद्रवा दुर्बलाग्नेः पिडिकाः परविर्जयेत् ।।३६।। (सु.न.अ. ६)

Patients who have developed these ulcers in the rectum , region of the heart , head , shoulders , back and vital parts of the body , associated with complications and who have poor digestive capacity are to be refused treatment.

# CHAPTER THREE

# Ayurveda Herbology for diabetes

## Ayurvedic Treatments

- *Udwartana* is a powder massage often used for slimming and treatment of obesity that can be done daily.
- *Dhanyamladhara* is often used in Ayurveda to combat obesity, inflammation, muscular pain, neuropathy, hemiplegia, and rheumatic complaints. It is derived from the word cereals (dhanya) and vinegar (amla). Dhanyamla involves preparation navara rice, horse gram, millet, citrus fruits, and dried ginger. During the treatment, the body is covered with this preparation and then by a heated cloth. The duration of the treatment is 45 to 50 minutes depending upon the condition of the patient.
- *Snehapana* is a process of full body internal and external lubrication via drinking ghee and animal fat oil as well as massaging the oil on without any other oral intake.
- *Abhyanga* is a warm oil massage. The oil is often premedicated with herbs for specific conditions.
- *Bashpasweda* is a steam chamber in which the patient sits while steam emanates from a boiling herbal decoction.
- *Vamana* (induced vomiting) is targeted to expel increased kapha dosha from the body.
- *Virechana* is the second procedure in the sequence of Panchakarma (Ayurveda Detoxification Program) that involves using plant medicines that have a laxative effect, mainly aimed at reducing pitta dosha and toxic accumulation in the gastrointestinal tract, liver, and gallbladder.

- *Yogavasti* is a type of medication given by enema, aiding in diminishing extra vata dosha present in the body. Vata is the force behind the elimination and retention of feces, urine, bile, and other excreta.
- *Shirodhara* is a form of Ayurveda therapy that involves gently pouring liquids over the forehead and can be one of the steps involved in Panchakarma.

## Ayurveda diet for diabetes

Needless to say, foods low in glycemic index must be included in the diet. Besides this, one must load up on green leafy vegetables. Omega 3 fatty acids, especially the ones alternatively known as brain fatty acids must be a part of your daily diet; these would include nuts and seeds like flaxseeds, walnuts et cetera. "Make sure that foods are also laxative in nature; therefore soak seeds and nuts before consuming as eating them as is may cause constipation. The idea is to keep your intestinal path clean and clear and avoid falling prey to constipation," shared Yogi Anoop. *Methi dana* works wonders for diabetics, from consuming *methi dana* sprouts to drinking fenugreek water the first thing in morning. Hemp seeds and ingredients like bitter gourd, *amla* and aloe vera have also been found effective in managing and controlling diabetes.

## Ayurveda Herbology for diabetes

1. **Rishyagandha** is the Natural Insulin Extract and have the properties which directly heals Beta Cells and make them repaired and promotes the secretion of insulin in the right amount. Withania Coagulans tends to the Herb Commonly Named Paneer Doda in General and in accordance to Ayurveda Aushadialya Rishyagandha contains the Healing Property which repairs the body Cells.
2. **False Kamani** contain glycoside amygdalin. When eaten, glycoside amygdalin will turn into prussic acid and this acid is the Natural Insulin Extract and have the properties which directly heals Beta Cells.
3. **Inderjoon:** the herb Gymnema Sylvestre has been used in traditional Indian medicine for many years now – among other things, it is claimed to help control diabetes and this is reported in Lab Tests that herb

Gymnema Sylvestrehas the properties to digest and decrease the absorption of excess blood sugar from the intestine.

4.  **Snow Mountain Garlic** is grown as well as native to the Kashmir region of India. It's grown in 1800 meters above sea levels in high altitudes, in an extremely dry and snowy area with very little oxygen availability. Himalayan Garlic is considered one of the purest varieties of garlic as it is grown in lack of industrial pollutants in the soil.

5.  **Khas Khas Root** is also used for cooling purposes, flavoring sharbats, and making mats, hand fans and sedative effect and aids in the treatment of emotional outbursts, such as anger, anxiety, epileptic and hysteric attacks, restlessness, nervousness, etc.

6.  **Turmeric** is thought to have many medicinal properties including strengthening the overall energy of the body, relieving gas, dispelling worms, improving digestion, regulating menstruation, dissolving gallstones, and relieving arthritis.

# CHAPTER FOUR

# RISHYAGANDHA A Comprehensive Source of Natural Insulin

**Scientific Name: Withania Coagulans or Indian Rennet**
   **Aushadhialya Reference: Rishyagandha**
   **General References: Paneer Doda / Rishyagandha**
   **Other economic significant: Ashutosh Booti**

## ABSTRACT

Withania Coagulans is the Natural Insulin Extract and have the properties which directly heals Beta Cells and make them repaired and promotes the secretion of insulin in the right amount. Withania Coagulans tends to the Herb Commonly Named Paneer Doda in General and in accordance to Ayurveda Aushadialya Rishyagandha contains the Healing Property which repairs the body Cells.

## BACKGROUND

Commonly known as Paneer doda, the herb Withania coagulans has been used in traditional Indian medicine for many years now – among other things, it is claimed to help control diabetes.

## METHODS

The Extract of 40mg Withania Coagulans was separated from thermal desorption used electric and field to measure the mass of the Sample under Mass Spectrometry and components extracted here founded similar components of Natural Insulin (Short Acting Insulin) and outcome has no toxic Element in the sample.

## LAB TESTING

When tested, the compounds were found which increases insulin secretion by mouse pancreatic cells, we found here Withania contains the Natural Insulin Extracts. The herb promotes the depletion of blood sugar with improvement in glucose utilization and carbohydrate metabolism. It lowers the complication of hyperglycemia.

- Heals the Beta-Cells
- Burns Pancreas Fat
- Digests in 2 Hours

And further here are a few most important benefits of including it in your diet:

- **Respiratory Disorders**

It cures common cough, cold and flu easily. Regular consumption of Withania coagulans in winter reduces the chances of mucous formation and inflammation around the throat. It is also a good remedy for patients suffering from respiratory disorders like asthma and bronchitis.

## RESULTS

In our research, When tested, the compounds were found which increases insulin secretion by mouse pancreatic cells, we found here Withania contains the Natural Insulin Extracts and hereby further healing properties which directly Effects Beta Cells to make them repaired and promotes the secretion of insulin in the right amount. The herb promotes the depletion of blood sugar with improvement in glucose utilization and carbohydrate metabolism. It lowers the complication of hyperglycemia.

The Usage of Rishyagandha Improves the Physical Stamina and gives the strong Immune system. The usage of anti-diabetic drugs and insulin is lowered on regular use of Paneer Dodi. Hence Panner Dodi is a safe and effective way to manage Diabetes Mellitus as a single supplement to synthetic anti-diabetic drugs.

## CONCLUSION

The Core benefits of Withania Coagulans Came out in our Research are facts of the contains Natural Insulin Extract and have the properties which directly heals Beta Cells and make them repaired and promotes the secretion of insulin in the right amount and on the other side helps in curing asthma, berries of this plants purify the blood which eases to clear acne, chewing of twigs helps to clean tooth, the paste of paneer Doda, when applied on wounds, speeds up the healing process, relieves stress, promote a sense of well-being, reduces body aches and improves physical stamina.

# CHAPTER FIVE

# SEA TROPICALS Developer of Natural Insulin

**Scientific Name: Lexzus Lexrica / Terminalia catappa**
**Aushadhialya Reference: False Kamani**
**General References: Samundri Kadwe Badam**
**Other economic significant: Sky Fruit**

## ABSTRACT

Sea Tropicals contain glycoside amygdalin. When eaten, glycoside amygdalin will turn into prussic acid and this acid is the Natural Insulin Extract and had the properties which directly heal

Beta Cells. False Kamani has the Healing Properties which directly heals the Immunity system of Human Body. Mainly Sea Tropical's Extract Produce Glycoside Amygdalin inside the stomach which is a silent Poison but source of the Natural Insulin as Beta-cells Uses the Amygdalin Poison to Secrete Insulin.

## BACKGROUND

Commonly known as False Kamni, the herb Terminalia catappa has been used in traditional Indian medicine for many years now – among other things, it is claimed to help control diabetes and this is reported in Lab Tests that Terminalia catappa is the source of natural Insulin.

## METHODS

The Extract of 40mg Terminalia catappa was separated from thermal desorption used electric and field to measure the mass of the Sample under Mass Spectrometry and components extracted here founded The Silent

Poison and the extract similar to Natural Insulin's contain glycoside amygdalin.

## LAB TESTING

When tested, the compounds were found with contain glycoside amygdalin Extract Produce Glycoside Amygdalin inside the stomach which is a silent Poison but source of the Natural Insulin as Beta-cells Uses the Amygdalin Poison to Secrete Insulin.

## RESULTS

In our research, When tested, the compounds were found contain glycoside amygdalinwhich increases insulin secretion by mouse pancreatic cells, we found here contain glycoside amygdalin is the input poison that is used by beta-cells to produce insulin.

## CONCLUSION

The Core benefits of herb Terminalia catappa Came out in our Research are facts of the contains Natural Insulin Extract and have the contain glycoside amygdalin which directly used by Beta Cells promotes the secretion of insulin in the right amount

On the other side helps in Fat Burning, purify the blood which eases to clear acne.

# CHAPTER SIX

# GYMNEMA SYLVESTRE
# Immune and Cell Repairing

**Scientific Name: Gymnema Sylvestre**
**Aushadhialya Reference: GurmarBooti**
**General References: Inder Joon / Gurmar**
**Other economic significant: Periploca**

## ABSTRACT

It's also called gurmar, which is Hindi for "destroyer of sugar" Gymnema contains substances that decrease the absorption of sugar from the intestine. Gymnema may also increase the amount of insulin in the body and increase the growth of cells in the pancreas, which is the place in the body where insulin is made.

## BACKGROUND

Commonly known as Inderjoon, the herb Gymnema Sylvestre has been used in traditional Indian medicine for many years now – among other things, it is claimed to help control diabetes and this is reported in Lab Tests that herb Gymnema Sylvestrehas the properties to digest and decrease the absorption of excess blood sugar from the intestine.

## METHODS

The Extract of 40mg Gymnema Sylvestre was separated from thermal desorption used electric and field to measure the mass of the Sample under Mass Spectrometry and components extracted here founded The Gymnema Sylvestre has higher InsulinInteraction Rating and moderate o increase the amount of insulin in the body and increase the growth of cells in the pancreas.

## RESULTS

In our research, When tested, the components under Gymnema Sylvestre have the properties to dedigest and decrease the absorption of excess blood sugar from the intestine.

# CHAPTER SEVEN

# SNOW MOUNTAIN GARLIC
## Boiler that boils blood sugar

**Scientific Name:Allium sativum/ Himalyan Garlic**

**Aushadhialya Reference:Ek Tehuni Lehsun**

**General References:Kashmiri Lahsun**

**Other economic significant: Sky Fruit**

### ABSTRACT

Snow Mountain Garlic, also known as Kashmiri Lahsun or Himalayan Garlic or Ek Pothi Lahsun is a specific variety of garlic found in the Himalayan region.In Ayurveda, it is a highly revered medicine and considered very effective alone for many ailments including Lung Cancer, Diabetes and Asthma.

### BACKGROUND

Snow Mountain Garlic is grown as well as native to the Kashmir region of India. It's grown in 1800 meters above sea levels in high altitudes, in an extremely dry and snowy area with very little oxygen availability. Himalayan Garlic is considered one of the purest varieties of garlic as it is grown in lack of industrial pollutants in the soil.

### METHODS

The Extract of 40mg Gymnema Sylvestre was separated from thermal desorption used electric and field to measure the mass of the Sample under Mass Spectrometry and components extracted here foundedSnow Mountain Garlic is considered to have antimicrobial, antibacterial, antifungal and antiviral properties. It contains a compound named allicin, which gives the garlic a pungent smell. This compound has antioxidant and antibacterial properties. Himalayan Garlic is also rich in Copper, Selenium, Phosphorous, Manganese, Sulphur, Vitamin B6, B1 and C, Calcium.

## RESULTS

In our research, When tested, the components under Snow Mountain Garlic is considered to have antimicrobial, antibacterial, antifungal and antiviral properties. It contains a compound named allicin, which gives the garlic a pungent smell. This compound has antioxidant and antibacterial properties. Himalayan Garlic is also rich in Copper, Selenium, Phosphorous, Manganese, Sulphur, Vitamin B6, B1 and C, Calcium.

## LAB TESTING

When tested, the compounds were found with contain Allicin, when combined with Vitamin B thiamine, triggers the pancreas to make insulin. And further Here are a few most important benefits of including it in your diet:

**Diabetes:** It controls and reduces blood sugar levels. Allicin, when combined with Vitamin B thiamine, triggers the pancreas to make insulin.

**Heart Diseases:** Kashmiri Lehsun is excellent for heart diseases. It strengthens the cardiovascular system and cures heart troubles. It helps maintains the hearts normal functions. Cholesterol is considered one of the main reason for many heart diseases. Snow mountain garlic reduces the possibility of coronary diseases by reducing cholesterol levels. It reduces LDL Cholesterol and triglycerides in the blood. It prevents the formation of the blood clot and lowers blood thickness and density which lowers the possibility of strokes and heart blockage. It is also used as a blood-thinning agent.

**Hypertension:** It reduces systolic and diastolic blood pressure. Hydrogen Sulphide found in garlic relaxes the muscles and limits the blood pressure in a healthy range. It is especially beneficial for Hypertension (HBP).

**Cancer Treatment:** It is best used as a medicine for cancer treatment. It stops the multiplication of cancer cells and reduces the possibility of cancer from developing. It is useful in curing Pancreas, Colon, Prostate, Lung and Stomach Cancer. Only 3 to 4 cloves of garlic a day, if consumed on a regular basis, can help fight lung diseases and cancer.

**Respiratory Disorders**

It cures common cough, cold and flu easily. Regular consumption of Kashmiri Lehsun in winter reduces the chances of mucous formation and inflammation around the throat. It is also a good remedy for patients suffering from respiratory disorders like asthma and bronchitis.

**Brain Tumour**: It rejuvenates the brain and helps cure brain tumours. Research shows that the sulphur content of Himalayan Garlic combats Glioblastoma which is a kind of a brain tumour.

**Immunity**: It increases immunity. It can be used as a regular immunity boosting supplement.

**Digestive Disorders**: It helps reduce digestive disorders like acid reflux and indigestion but only as preventive medicine. If you suffer from chronic acidity, gastritis, and heartburn, it is not recommended to consume Himalayan Garlic.

**Constipation**: It also regulates and improves bowel movement. It is also helpful in relieving constipation.

# CHAPTER EIGHT

# PERENNIAL GRASS Toxin Remover

**Scientific Name:Chrysopogon zizanioides/ Vetiveria Bory (vetivergrass)**
**Aushadhialya Reference:**
**General References:Khus Khus Roots**
**Other economic significant:Poaceae**

## ABSTRACT

Vetiveria zizanioides, also known as khas khas, khas or khus grass, is native to India.

## BACKGROUND

Khas Khas is also used for cooling purposes, flavoring sharbats, and making mats, hand fans etc.

## METHODS

Its main chemical components are benzoic acid, vetiverol, furfurol, a and b-vetivone, vetivene and vetivenyl vetivenate. The chemical components of the oil obtained from the plant is benzoic acid, furfurol, vetivene, vetivenyl vetivenate, terpinen-4-ol, 5-epiprezizane, Khusimene, a-muurolene, Khusimone, Calacorene, ß-humulene, a-longipinene, ?-selinene, d-selinene,d-cadinene, valencene, Calarene,-gurjunene, a-amorphene, Epizizanal, 3-epizizanol, Khusimol, Iso-khusimol, Valerenol, ß-vetivone, a-vetivone, vetivazulene.

## LAB TESTING

When tested, the compounds were found It has anti-inflammatory and antiseptic effects that provide relief from inflammations in circulatory system and nervous system.

## RESULTS

In our research, When tested, khus khus has sedative effect and aids in the treatment of emotional outbursts, such as anger, anxiety, epileptic and hysteric attacks, restlessness, nervousness, etc..

# CHAPTER NINE

# CURCUMA The Natural Antiseptic

**Scientific Name:***Curcuma/ Terra Merita*
**Aushadhialya Reference:***Haridra*
**General References:Indian yellow saffron**
**Other economic significant:Turmeric**

## ABSTRACT

Turmeric is a product of *Curcuma longa*, a rhizomatous herbaceous perennial plant belonging to the ginger family. More than 100 components have been isolated from turmeric. The main component of the root is a volatile oil, containing turmerone, and there are other coloring agents called curcuminoids in turmeric. Curcuminoids consist of curcumin demethoxycurcumin, 5'-methoxycurcumin, and dihydrocurcumin, which are found to be natural antioxidants

## BACKGROUND

Turmeric is used as an herbal medicine for rheumatoid arthritis, chronic anterior uveitis, conjunctivitis, skin cancer, small pox, chicken pox, wound healing, urinary tract infections, and liver ailments.

Turmeric is thought to have many medicinal properties including strengthening the overall energy of the body, relieving gas, dispelling worms, improving digestion, regulating menstruation, dissolving gallstones, and relieving arthritis.

Indians use turmeric, in addition to its Ayurvedic applications, to purify blood and remedy skin conditions. Turmeric is currently used in the formulation of several sunscreens. Several multinational companies are involved in making face creams based on turmeric.

Turmeric is a well-documented treatment for various respiratory conditions (e.g., asthma, bronchial hyperactivity, and allergy), as well as for liver disorders, anorexia, rheumatism, diabetic wounds, runny nose, cough, and sinusitis.

## METHODS

The Extract of 40mg Terminalia catappa was separated from thermal desorption used electric and field to measure the mass of the Sample under Mass Spectrometry and components extracted here founded turmeric is a potent antioxidant, anti-inflammatory, anti-mutagenic, antimicrobial, and anticancer agent.

## LAB TESTING

When tested, the compounds were found with contain turmeric has strong antimicrobial properties. The growth of histamine-producing bacteria (*Vibrio parahaemolyticus*, *Bacillus cereus*, *Pseudomonas aeruginosa*, and *Proteus mirabilis*) was inhibited by garlic and turmeric extracts at a 5% concentration.a potent antioxidant, anti-inflammatory, antimutagenic, antimicrobial, and anticancer agent.

The anticancer activities of turmeric include inhibiting cell proliferation and inducing apoptosis of cancer cells. Arturmerone, which is isolated from turmeric, induced apoptosis in human leukemia Molt 4B and HL-60 cells by fragmenting DNA to oligonucleosome-sized fragments, a known step in the process of apoptosis

that turmeric extract repressed the production and secretion of hepatitis B surface antigen from HepG 2.2.15 cells, an activity that is mediated through the enhancement of cellular accumulation of p53 protein by transactivating the transcription of the p53 gene as well as increasing the stability of the p53 protein

## RESULTS

In our research, When tested, the compounds were found contain turmeric has strong antimicrobial properties. The growth of histamine-producing bacteria (*Vibrio parahaemolyticus*, *Bacillus cereus*, *Pseudomonas aeruginosa*, and *Proteus mirabilis*) was inhibited by garlic and turmeric extracts at a 5% concentration. a potent antioxidant, anti-inflammatory, antimutagenic, antimicrobial, and anticancer agent.

## CONCLUSION

The Core benefits of herb Terminalia catappa Came out in our Research are facts of the contains Natural Insulin Extract and have the contain contain turmeric has strong antimicrobial properties. The growth of histamine-producing bacteria *(Vibrio parahaemolyticus, Bacillus cereus, Pseudomonas aeruginosa,* and *Proteus mirabilis)* was inhibited by garlic and turmeric extracts at a 5% concentration. a potent antioxidant, anti-inflammatory, antimutagenic, antimicrobial, and anticancer agent.

On the other side helps in Fat Burning, purify the blood which eases to clear acne.

Turmeric acts as a digestive stimulant. As a dietary supplement, it favorably enhanced the activities of pancreatic lipase, chymotrypsin, and amylase. Moreover, turmeric mixed with other spices such as coriander, red chili, black pepper, and cumin brought about a pronounced stimulation of bile flow and bile acid secretion.

# Conclusion

It has been narrated in Ayurveda that, the long periods of physical inactivity, laziness, sleeping for long hours, excess use of food which is heavy to digest like dairy products, aquatic and marshy animals, sugar/jaggery preparations, fresh grains etc. and similar foods that increase kapha are generalized causes of prameha \ diabetes mellitus. Diabetes is a metabolic disease that occurs when your blood sugar also known as blood glucose level is too high. The term high blood glucose is also known a HYPERGLYCAEMIA

Patients with type 2 diabetes may inquire about current complementary and alternative therapies available for the treatment of their disease. Awareness of such modalities is necessary for effective patient counseling and care. The benefits of offering a wide array of treatment options include possible reduction of HbA1c and of comorbidities with adjunct use of supplements and mind–body practices.

# The Key Benefits Of Dr. Glucofit

Outcome Key Benefits clinically tested and proven:

- Helps to regenerate insulin-producing cells (beta cells).
- Mission zero diabetes with care.
- Increases insulin production and helps reduce sugar cravings.
- Prevents sugar spike (insulin resistance) and delays glucose absorption from intestines.
- Aids in regulating and Controls sugar level in diabetic patients.
- Helps in the purification of blood.
- Helps in boosting metabolism and improves immunity.
- Useful in case of indigestion and intestinal worms.
- Has antioxidant properties and protects cells from harmful free radicals.
- Also acts as an anti-allergic, particularly for skin allergies and urticaria.
- Balances kapha and pitta dosha.
- Strengthens pancreas.
- Regulating blood sugar levels.
- Helps in maintaining normal blood glucose level.